THE HISTORY OF
WESTMI

Ⓗ ow old is Westmin... g-
end places the fou... h
century, but we cannot know if this is true. What is certain is
that around AD 960 the bishop of London, Dunstan (FIG. 1), established here a group of twelve monks, so we can be sure that God
has been worshipped on this site for over a thousand years.

Those early monks came to a place then known as 'Thorney Island', an isolated, marshy area along the banks of the Thames, very different from the bustling city that is Westminster today.

The early monastic community enjoyed the support of King Edgar (ruled 957–75), who granted land, thus forging the close links between Crown and Church that run

1 St Dunstan from the late fourteenth-century Litlyngton Missal

through the Abbey's history. A century later King Edward (FIG. 2) established his palace on Thorney Island and began to enlarge and richly to endow the small monastic community there. He provided the monks with additional lands and built a major stone church, which was dedicated in December 1065. Monas-

tic churches at this time were often called 'minsters', and Edward's new church became known as the 'west minster' to distinguish it from St Paul's Cathedral (the 'east minster') further along the banks of the Thames. Nothing of King Edward's church remains above ground, but some of its foundations have been found below the present church and show that it was a building of

2 St Edward the Confessor from the Litlyngton Missal

3 The south transept and the cloister fountain

considerable size. From its depiction in the Bayeux Tapestry we know that it had a central tower, transepts and a lead-covered roof. King Edward was buried here in January 1066.

Edward's reputation as a holy man transformed the history of Westminster Abbey. In 1161 he was canonised by the Pope and became St Edward the Confessor (a confessor being someone who has lived a holy life, 'confessing' the Christian faith). His body was transferred to a new shrine in the Abbey, and Westminster became a place of pilgrimage.

Most of the church we see today was built on the orders of Henry III between 1245 and 1272. Henry's intention was to provide a magnificent new shrine for the Confessor's remains within a new abbey church built in the latest French Gothic style of architecture. In fact the building is a mixture of French and English elements. The eastern end with its apse and radiating chapels, the use of flying buttresses for structural support and the round or 'rose' windows in the transepts (FIGS 3 and 4) are all features of the French style. The long nave and widely projecting transepts are characteristically English. A series of master masons supervised the building, which was constructed mainly of French stone from Caen and English marble from Purbeck in Dorset. By 1269 the whole of the quire, transepts and eastern end of the church, together with the new shrine of St Edward, a small portion of the nave and the chapter house, were complete. However, most of the nave of Edward the Confessor's church remained attached to this new work for over a century. Work on rebuilding the nave continued gradually from 1376 until 1498, but the vaulting was not complete until 1517. Even then the exterior remained unfinished until the addition in 1745 of the west towers, designed by Nicholas Hawksmoor.

Throughout the medieval building work at Westminster the monks continued to follow the monastic Rule of St Benedict, devoting their lives to worship, manual labour and study. The ancillary buildings required in any monastery were gradually added, and thanks to royal patronage Westminster became one of the wealthiest and most important monasteries in the country. It comes as a surprise to realise that for most of the Middle Ages the monastic community here numbered only about fifty monks. There were additional lay brethren and servants, however, so the monastic precinct, enclosed by its high wall (parts of which still survive), had something of the feel of a village. Monasteries were an essential part of medieval life, a place where Christians could strive to live closer to God than was possible in the outside world. Monks and nuns committed themselves to a life of poverty, chastity and obedience to the Rule of their order. They prayed at fixed times during the day and night at services, which became known as the monastic 'offices'.

Life changed for ever at Westminster during the reign of Henry VIII. As part of the religious turmoil known as the Reformation, which dominated church life during the sixteenth century, the monasteries in England and Wales were closed down, or 'dissolved'. Westminster was dissolved (as a monastic Abbey) in 1540, but communities of clergy continued to live and worship here, though the next twenty years in particular were ones of upheaval and change. Finally, in 1560, Queen Elizabeth I re-founded the Abbey as a 'collegiate church', to be governed by a group of clergy (known as the Dean and Chapter) whose principal duty was the daily worship of God. To assist in this a musical foundation of organist, choristers and singing men was established, and there was provision for the education of forty scholars too. These were the forerunners of the present-day Queen's Scholars of Westminster School, which still occupies premises adjacent to the Abbey but now has around 750 pupils. The new foundation was a Royal Peculiar, a church outside the normal governance structure of the Church of England and answerable only to the Sovereign.

During the period known as the Commonwealth, in the mid-seventeenth century, the clergy were ejected from the Abbey, but the collegiate foundation was re-established at the Restoration of the monarchy in 1660 and worship was resumed. Although the services were those of the Church of England, the pattern of daily morning and evening prayer recalled, albeit in a simpler form, the monastic offices that were recited at Westminster for the first 600 years of its existence. Another example of the remarkable continuity in the Abbey's life is the continued use of the title 'Westminster Abbey', even though the church has long ceased to be a monastery. The Abbey's formal title since 1560 has been The Collegiate Church of St Peter in Westminster.

It is safe to say that anyone who lived here in the last days of the monastery in the 1540s would recognise the exterior of the Abbey today. Inside, however, the Reformation in particular brought many changes. Burial in the Abbey (a privilege largely confined to royalty and a few of the aristocracy in the Middle Ages) became much more common, and the side chapels in particular – stripped of their medieval altars and furnishings – began to fill with tombs. By the eighteenth century the Abbey had established a reputation as the place of burial and commemoration for the great and famous, though many other people were buried here as well. More than 3,000 people are interred or commemorated in the church and cloisters, and there are some 600 tombs, monuments and memorials, making the Abbey's collection of monumental sculpture the most significant in the country.

4 North transept rose window

Sir Christopher Wren was the first architect to be appointed as 'Surveyor of the Fabric' in 1698, with general responsibility for the upkeep of the buildings. Since then there have been several major programmes of restoration, most recently a complete cleaning of the interior in the years following the Second World War and a major programme of restoration of the exterior, which ended in 1995. The care of the Abbey is, however, a continuous task of great importance and complexity.

THE NAVE

THE PRESENT NAVE took several centuries to complete. The rebuilding begun by Henry III extended a little west of the quire screen, but for a hundred years after that the new Gothic work was joined to the eleventh-century nave of the Confessor's abbey. Work resumed in 1376, at the end of the reign of Edward III, but using the same Gothic architectural style of Henry III's church to give the nave a harmony of design and atmosphere. If you cast your eye up to the vault (102 feet above the floor), you can only wonder at the skill and dedication of the craftsmen who laboured on this building. The distinctive chandeliers were a gift to the Abbey in 1966 to mark 900th anniversary of the dedication of Edward the Confessor's church.

At the west end of the nave is the Grave of the Unknown Warrior (A; FIG. 5), whose body was brought back from the battlefields of the First World War to be buried here 'among the kings'. One hundred holders of the Victoria Cross lined the nave as a guard of honour at the service at which the Unknown Warrior was buried on 11 November 1920, which was attended by

5 Grave of the Unknown Warrior

King George V and Queen Mary. The grave contains soil from the battlefields of France and is covered by a slab of Belgian marble. Surrounded by red poppies (the flower that grew on the battlefields of Flanders), it is one of the most poignant memorials in the Abbey and a place of pilgrimage for people from all over the world. Visiting heads of state and other dignitaries pay their respects here. The Congressional Medal, conferred on the Unknown Warrior by the United States of America, hangs nearby.

On a side pillar to the left of the west door is the magnificent portrait of Richard II (FIG. 6), made at the end of the fourteenth century and the earliest known contemporary likeness of an English monarch. Nearby, in the centre of the nave floor, is a memorial to Sir Winston Churchill (1874–1965), prime minister and wartime leader.

On pillars in the centre of the nave are two icons of Christ and the Virgin Mary by Sergei Federov. Placed here in 1994 amid the many memorials to human endeavour and achievement, they are reminders of the Abbey's primary mission to worship God and to proclaim the good news of his loving purposes for the human race. Before you leave, you may wish to say a prayer here or light a candle in thanksgiving for your visit.

Further east is the stone screen which in all monastic churches separated the nave from the quire (**B**; FIG. 7). The present screen was designed in 1834, but has the masonry of the original medieval screen at its core. Above is the organ, which has been developed from one built in 1727 for the coronation

6 Portrait of Richard II

7 Quire screen and monuments

of George II and Queen Caroline. It now has about 7,000 pipes, some of which are so long that they lie horizontally above the vault of the aisles. To the left of the screen arch is the monument to Sir Isaac Newton (1642–1727), who is buried just in front of it. The graves of Charles Darwin (1809–82) and Stephen Hawking (1942–2018) and memorial stones of other prominent scientists are nearby.

To the left of the quire screen is the north quire aisle, where a number of composers are buried or commemorated. They include Henry Purcell (1659–95) and his teacher John Blow

8 Coronation Chair

(1649–1708), both celebrated organists of the Abbey. Two campaigners against the slave trade are also remembered in this aisle: William Wilberforce (1759–1833) and Thomas Clarkson (1760–1846).

You will return to the nave at the end of your tour. Before leaving the abbey through the west door, you will have an opportunity to view the Coronation Chair (I; FIG 8), which is in St George's Chapel at the west end of the nave. The chair has been used at every corona-

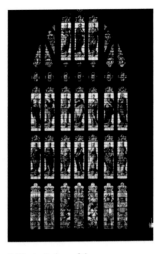

9 West window of the nave

tion since at least that of Henry IV in the fourteenth century. It was made on the order of Edward I to contain the Stone of Scone (used when the Scottish kings were crowned), which he had captured from the Scots in 1296 and brought back to Westminster. The chair was originally decorated with coloured patterns of birds, foliage and animals, all on a gilt background. Sadly most of this has been lost, and because the chair was left unprotected from the public for many centuries it has suffered much damage, including carved graffiti. The Stone of Scone was originally kept beneath the chair's seat, but in 1996 the government ordered its return to Scotland. For a coronation service, the chair is moved to a position in front of the high altar.

When leaving the Abbey at the end of your tour, you might stop to look outside at the statues of twentieth-century martyrs (J), which were placed in previously empty niches above the west door in 1998. From the left they depict: Maximilian Kolbe, Poland (d. 1941); Manche Masemola, South Africa (d. 1928); Janani Luwum, Uganda (d. 1977); Grand Duchess Elizabeth of Russia (d. 1918); Martin Luther King, USA (d. 1968); Oscar Romero, El Salvador (d. 1980); Dietrich Bonhoeffer, Germany (d. 1945); Esther John, Pakistan (d. 1960); Lucian Tapiedi, Papua New Guinea (d. 1942); and Wang Zhiming, China (d. 1972). Above the west door is the great window, filled in 1735 with coloured glass depicting Abraham, Isaac, Jacob and fourteen prophets (FIG. 9).

THE QUIRE AND SANCTUARY

THE QUIRE, to the west of the crossing, is where the monastic offices were chanted. No trace remains of the medieval choir stalls, which were removed in the eighteenth century, and the present ones date from the mid-nineteenth century. They provide seating for the Abbey's clergy, choir and lay officers. Stalls are also assigned to the high commissioners of the Commonwealth countries, Canada, Australia, New Zealand and South Africa having permanently named places.

The daily services at Westminster Abbey are sung by a choir of about twenty-two boys and twelve lay vicars (the name given to the men of the choir). The choristers are educated at the Westminster Abbey Choir School in Dean's Yard, where their daily timetable accommodates both their singing duties and their general education.

The focal point of the sanctuary is the high altar and its screen (FIG. 10), designed by Sir George Gilbert Scott in 1867. The altar

10 High altar

11 Cosmati pavement

is decorated with embroidered 'frontals' in colours that change according to the seasons of the Church's year. If you visit during Lent or Holy Week, you will find the elaborate gilded screen covered by much plainer linen hangings.

In front of the altar is one of the Abbey's finest treasures – a pavement dating from 1268 (FIG. 11). The type of decoration used is known as Cosmati work, after the Italian family who developed the technique of inlaying intricate designs made up of small pieces of coloured marble and glass into a plain marble ground. This is the finest example in northern Europe, and the pattern depicts symbolically the creation and the end of the world. Another such pavement survives in the Chapel of St Edward the Confessor behind the altar screen. On the north side of the sanctuary are three notable thirteenth-century tombs, and on the south side is the tomb of Anne of Cleves (1516–57), fourth (and divorced) queen of Henry VIII, and the only one of his six wives buried in the Abbey.

12 The *Liber Regalis* is a fourteenth-century coronation service book

   This is also the area where coronations are held. Although aspects of this ancient ceremony have changed through the centuries, the main form of the service has remained the same. The Coronation Chair (SEE FIG. 8) is placed facing the high altar, and the monarch sits in it to be anointed with oil (the most solemn part of the ceremony) and then crowned. A raised dais is constructed in the lantern, and on this is set a second throne in which the newly crowned monarch is solemnly seated (thereby taking possession of the realm) to receive the people's homage. The most recent coronation, that of Queen Elizabeth II in 1953, was the first to be televised. It was attended by more than 8,000 people, many of whom were seated in specially built galleries high up in the transepts and elsewhere.

THE NORTH AMBULATORY

From the quire turn into the north ambulatory (from the Latin word *ambulare*, meaning 'to walk'), which will take you to the eastern end of the church. On your left is a large monument to General James Wolfe (1727–59), who was killed leading the capture of Quebec. During the First World War a number of Canadian regiments laid up their flags or 'colours' on this monument. After the Armistice the Canadian government asked that two flags should remain as a reminder of Canada's help to the United Kingdom in her time of need.

Next to Wolfe's monument is the entrance to an aisle that once housed three separate chapels. It now contains many monuments, the most famous being a remarkable work by the French sculptor Louis François Roubiliac dating from 1761 (FIG. 13). Commemorating Lady Elizabeth Nightingale (1704–31), it shows her husband attempting in vain to protect her from a skeletal figure of Death, who bursts from his cavern to claim her. At the far end of the aisle is the imposing monument to Henry, Lord Norris (1525?–1601), and his wife, Margaret (d. 1599), favourites of Queen Elizabeth I. Their six sons kneel around the monument: Edward, the only one to outlive his father, is shown looking upwards, while the others bow their heads in prayer.

13 Death from the Nightingale monument

Returning to the ambulatory, you pass the two-storey chapel built by John Islip, abbot of Westminster from 1500 until 1532. Islip's abbacy saw much building work at Westminster: the new Lady Chapel was begun, the nave completed and the west window (though not its present stained glass) installed. The lower chantry chapel, where Islip is buried, can be seen through the stone screen; the upper chapel is now the Florence Nightingale Chapel and contains several nursing memorials. Next to the Islip Chapel is St John the Baptist's Chapel, containing the tallest memorial in the Abbey. It commemorates Henry Carey,

Lord Hunsdon (c.1525–96), Lord Chamberlain to Elizabeth I.

A wooden staircase on the right gives access to the Chapel of St Edward the Confessor, which lies to the east of the high altar and is separated from it by a stone screen built around 1440. From the ambulatory you can glimpse in the middle of the chapel the shrine of St Edward (c.1005–66) (FIG. 14), which dates from 1269 and was an integral part of Henry III's plans for rebuilding the church. It consists of a stone base (containing the coffin) surmounted by a wooden canopy, and was once lavishly decorated with gold and jewels, many given as thank-offerings by the thousands of pilgrims who came here to pray during the Middle Ages. When the monastery was closed in 1540, this activity ceased and the shrine was dismantled, but during the reign of Mary I the monks briefly returned to the Abbey and the shrine was reassembled in its present form. St Edward is now the only major English saint whose body still rests in its medieval shrine. His chapel is at the very heart of the Abbey, but is a small, enclosed space with a delicate thirteenth-century Italian floor, and for this reason public access is now restricted.

14 Shrine of St Edward the Confessor

Surrounding St Edward's shrine are important tombs of medieval kings and queens, and these can be seen as you walk round the ambulatory. The entrance into the Confessor's Chapel passes between the very plain tomb of Edward I (1239–1307), nicknamed 'Long-shanks' because of his height, and the more elaborate tomb of Henry III (1207–72) (FIG. 15), who was responsible for the thirteenth-century rebuilding of the Abbey. Further along the ambulatory is the tomb of Eleanor of Castile (1241–90) (FIG. 16), first wife of Edward I. He was so distraught by her death that as her body was carried from Lincoln to Westminster he erected a memorial cross at each place where the procession rested. The

15 Henry III

16 Eleanor of Castille

last of these was built at Charing Cross, not far from the Abbey.

The most lavish royal burial in the Confessor's Chapel was that of Henry V (1387–1422) (FIG. 17), whose tomb stands at the east end of the chapel. Above it was constructed a chapel where the monks of Westminster prayed for his soul, and as you move towards the end of the north ambulatory you pass beneath the chapel. Look up to admire its elaborate structure and to see the carvings of Henry V on horseback and at his coronation.

To your left, alongside the entrance to St Paul's Chapel, is the tomb of Sir Lewis Robessart, Lord Bourgchier (d. 1430). It was restored in the 1960s, but its bright colours are a reminder that the interior of the medieval abbey church would have been richly decorated throughout.

17 Henry V

THE LADY CHAPEL

Y OU ARE NOW AT THE EASTERN END of the church, where a flight of steps leads to the Lady Chapel, which, as the name suggests, is dedicated to the Blessed Virgin Mary, mother of Jesus Christ. The chapel is also called King Henry VII's Chapel, after the king who ordered its construction from 1503 onwards. Henry VII (1457–1509), the first of the Tudor monarchs, conceived the chapel as a burial place for his predecessor Henry VI, whom he tried unsuccessfully to have canonised. Henry VI remained buried at Windsor and Henry VII, his wife and many of his successors were buried in the chapel. Henry made meticulous plans for it, left instructions in his will for its subsequent use and lavished huge sums of money on its construction and furnishings; he died before his chapel was dedicated in 1512. The chapel is virtually a church in itself, with a spectacular nave flanked by enclosed aisles to north and south. Its construction was a final flowering of pre-Reformation art and religious devotion at Westminster before the dissolution of the monastery by Henry VIII in 1540.

A doorway to the left at the top of the steps leads to the north aisle. It is dominated by the elaborate tomb of Elizabeth I (1533–1603) (C; FIG. 18), but is also the burial place of Mary I (1516–58), Elizabeth's half-sister and her predecessor as queen. Mary

18 Queen Elizabeth I

19 *King Henry VII's Lady Chapel*

remained a Roman Catholic and, on succeeding to the throne in 1553, restored the English church's allegiance to Rome and re-established a Benedictine community at Westminster. But her reign lasted only five years, and Elizabeth I reversed these changes, establishing a reformed Church of England under the authority of the monarch but grounded in the ancient doctrines and practices of the undivided Church.

Although Mary has no monument of her own, part of the Latin inscription on Elizabeth's tomb reads: *Partners both in throne and grave, here rest we two sisters, Elizabeth and Mary, in the hope of one Resurrection.* The burial place of these two queens – Elizabeth above and Mary below – divided in life by their religious convictions but in death resting together in Christian hope, provides a fitting setting for an inscription carved in the floor in 1977 to commemorate all those 'divided at the Reformation by different convictions who laid down their lives for Christ and conscience sake'.

Elaborate bronze gates decorated with Tudor royal badges such as the rose and the portcullis protect the entrance to the nave of the Lady Chapel (**D**; FIG. 19). Once inside, the eye of the visitor is immediately drawn to the roof with its intricate and finely detailed fan vaulting. The carved pendants may seem to defy gravity, but the roof is actually built of interlocking pieces of stone that fit together like a jigsaw puzzle. The perfection of its beauty and artistry is breathtaking.

Below the vault the chapel's walls consist of more glass than stonework, adding to the stunning architectural effect. Sadly only fragments of the original stained glass survive. The heraldic west window and the windows in the small side chapels at the east end (1995–7) commemorate benefactors who helped to restore the Abbey in the twentieth century. The central east window (2000), by Alan Younger, celebrates the Blessed Virgin Mary and is flanked by windows by Hughie O'Donoghue installed in 2013.

A remarkable survival, since such things were particularly vulnerable to attack during the Reformation, is the series of statues of saints that runs round the chapel at the level beneath the windows. Ninety-four of the original 107 statues are intact.

The Lady Chapel was built for use by the monks, and many of the oak seats or 'stalls' lining the chapel on each side are original. The undersides of the seats have carved decorations called *misericords* (from the Latin word for 'mercy'). They gave some support to the monks when they stood during long services, and even though the misericords were generally hidden from view, the carvings are very elaborate.

20 Fifteenth-century Italian altarpiece

At the dissolution of the monastery this chapel was stripped of its liturgical furnishings, and it was subsequently used only rarely until it became the chapel of the Most Honourable Order of the Bath in 1725. Membership of the Order is awarded for distinguished service in military or public life, and stalls in the chapel are allocated to the most senior members, who are called Knights Grand Cross. The banners of the current knights

21 Henry VII and Elizabeth of York

hang above the stalls, and heraldic plates provide a permanent record of each stall's occupants.

The chapel's altar dates from 1935, but is a reconstruction of the original, incorporating two pillars that survived the Reformation. A beautiful fifteenth-century painting of the Virgin and Child by the Italian artist Bartolomeo Vivarini acts as an altarpiece (FIG. 20). In front of the altar a stone commemorates the burial beneath the altar of Edward VI (1537–53). Other monarchs buried in vaults beneath the chapel's nave and aisles are James I, Charles II, William and Mary, Queen Anne and George II. Their names and dates are engraved on floor stones, but none has any proper monument.

The magnificent Renaissance tomb of Henry VII and his queen, Elizabeth of York (1465–1503) (FIG. 21), is of marble and gilt-bronze and the work of the Florentine sculptor Pietro Torrigiano. It is surrounded by an elaborate bronze screen, within which originally stood a small altar (dismantled at the Reformation) where the monks said mass for the repose of the king's and queen's souls.

The small chapel beyond is the Royal Air Force Memorial Chapel (FIG. 22), dedicated in 1947 in memory of the men who lost their lives in the Battle of Britain during the Second World War. A roll of honour containing the names of the 1,497 pilots and crew who died is kept here, and the striking window by Hugh Easton incorporates badges of the fighter squadrons who took part in the battle.

A small stone at the entrance to this chapel marks the original burial place of Oliver Cromwell (1599–1658). However, as a participant in the trial of King Charles I and a signatory to his death warrant, Cromwell was not destined to rest long in this

22 The Royal Air Force Memorial Chapel

royal burial place. Early in 1661, soon after the Restoration of the monarchy, his body was removed from its grave and hung from a gallows at Tyburn, the main place of public execution in London.

Henry VII probably always intended that the south aisle of the Lady Chapel should be the burial place of his mother. He could hardly have envisaged that in due course a granddaughter (Margaret, Countess of Lennox) and a great-granddaughter (Mary Queen of Scots) would rest here too! All three have notable tombs occupying the central space of the aisle.

Margaret Douglas, Countess of Lennox (1515–78), died in poverty and was buried here at the expense of her niece Elizabeth I. The tomb depicts the Countess's sons and daughters kneeling on either side of her effigy. The eldest son, Lord Darnley, married Mary Queen of Scots and was the father of James I, who commissioned this tomb after his accession to the English throne.

James's most extravagant tomb commission was for his mother, Mary Queen of Scots (1542–87) (**E**; FIG. 23), who spent the last nineteen years of her life imprisoned on the orders of her cousin Elizabeth I, by whom she was regarded as a dangerous rival claimant to the throne. Elizabeth eventually agreed to Mary's execution, insisting that she then be buried with great solemnity in Peterborough Cathedral. When Mary's son James VI of Scotland succeeded to the English throne as James I, he commissioned tombs at Westminster for both his mother and Elizabeth I. It is noticeable, however, that his mother's tomb, which dominates the centre of this aisle, is taller and more flamboyant than that of James' predecessor in the north aisle (SEE FIG. 18).

The third major tomb in this aisle is of Henry VII's mother, Margaret Beaufort, Countess of Richmond (1443–1509), a woman noted for both her Christian piety and her generous benefactions (she was the foundress of two colleges at Cambridge University). Lady Margaret's tomb, like that of her son in the nave of the Lady Chapel, is by Pietro Torrigiano – indeed the bronze effigy, with its beautiful praying hands, is reckoned by many to be his masterpiece.

23 Mary Queen of Scots

THE SOUTH AMBULATORY AND SOUTH TRANSEPT

A S YOU MOVE ALONG the south ambulatory, further glimpses may be had of the Confessor's Chapel between the tombs on your right. These tombs are of Edward III (1312–77) (FIG. 24), displaying bronze figures of his children on the side, and of Richard II (1367–1400) (FIG. 25) and his queen, Anne of Bohemia (1366–94). On the left are chapels (dedicated to St Nicholas and St Edmund respectively) that mirror those in the north ambulatory and which, like them, are filled with monuments.

24 Edward III

Continue along the ambulatory and into the south transept, famous as the site of Poets' Corner (**F**), which developed following the burial here of Geoffrey Chaucer (c.1343–1400) (FIG. 26). He was buried in the Abbey because he had served the royal household rather than on account of his writings, but in the sixteenth century his literary achievements came to be appreciated and his remains were transferred from their original grave to a new tomb on the east wall. The burial of Edmund Spenser (1553–99) followed shortly afterwards, and thus began the tradition of burying or commemorating poets, dramatists and other writers in this part of the Abbey. Over the centuries Poets' Corner has extended across most of the transept, and you do not need to look far on the walls or the floor to see familiar names, though it is not always clear whether someone is actually buried here or only commemorated. Among the many significant writers buried in

25 Richard II

26 Geoffrey Chaucer

Poets' Corner are Dr Samuel Johnson, Charles Dickens, Robert Browning, Alfred, Lord Tennyson, Thomas Hardy and Rudyard Kipling. Those only commemorated here include William Shakespeare (FIG. 27), Jane Austen, the Bronte sisters, Lewis Carroll, Henry James, T.S. Eliot and a number of the First World War poets. As floor space has become very limited, some commemorations are now also made in a stained-glass window above Chaucer's tomb.

Not all of those buried here are literary figures. The actors David Garrick (1716–99) and Sir Laurence Olivier (1907–1989) lie here, as does the composer George Frederick Handel (1685–1759). A curious stone in the middle of the transept marks the grave of Thomas Parr (d. 1635), who was said to have lived for 152 years!

Nearby is the entrance to The Queen's Diamond Jubilee Galleries (opened in 2018), where many of the Abbey's historic treasures are displayed (**K**). The Galleries occupy the eastern triforium, sixteen metres above your head, and offer splendid views down into the Abbey.

Before leaving the transept, be sure to see the two fine thirteenth-century wall paintings by the door leading into St Faith's Chapel. They were covered by monuments for nearly two hundred years and are remarkable survivals of the type of decorative art that would have been found throughout the church in the Middle Ages. St Faith's Chapel is set aside for prayer, and the Blessed Sacrament is reserved there. You are most welcome to go in and pray.

27 William Shakespeare

THE CLOISTERS AND THE MONASTIC PRECINCT

THE CLOISTERS (FIG. 28) were one of the busiest parts of the monastery. The monks undertook many daily tasks here: in the west walk the novices (trainee monks) received instruction; the north walk housed the library; the south walk led to the 'refectory' or dining room; and the east walk to the chapter house and dormitory.

In the octagonal Chapter House (G; FIG. 29), begun in 1250, the daily business of the monastery was discussed and tasks were allocated to the monks. The House of Commons sometimes met here too during the fourteenth century. A central column supports the roof vaulting, medieval paintings adorn the walls and the beautiful tiled pavement is original. After the dissolution of the monastery the Chapter House became a record office until its restoration in the middle of the nineteenth century. The stained glass is Victorian and twentieth century. There are

28 South cloister walk   **29** Chapter House vaulting

fine exterior views of the chapter house from the staircase leading to The Queen's Diamond Jubilee Galleries.

Returning through the vestibule to the cloister, notice a small
wooden door on the left. It is the oldest in England and has been
scientifically dated to about 1050. It was probably an important
door in Edward the Confessor's church and was later reduced
in size and re-used here.

The Pyx Chamber (**H**; FIG. 30) and the undercroft (not open
to the public at present) were built as a single space around
1070–80, making them the oldest parts of the Abbey and the
oldest rooms in London. The Pyx Chamber was later walled off
and became a royal treasury, acquiring a heavy oak door with
six locks. In the chamber was kept a 'pyx' or box containing stan-
dard pieces of gold and silver against which the current coinage
was tested each year.

If you walk through the 'dark cloister', another survival from
the eleventh century, you will see the enclosed garden in Little
Cloister. On certain days you can also visit College Garden, which
was originally the monastic infirmary garden and is thought to

30 Altar in the Pyx Chamber

have been continuously cultivated for more than 900 years.

Returning to the cloisters there are many more gravestones and memorials to be seen in the south and west cloisters. Three tombs of early Westminster abbots, placed close up to the wall in the south cloister walk, are the Abbey's oldest tombs. The effigy of Gilbert Crispin, abbot from 1085, is probably the oldest in the country. A modern memorial in the south cloister celebrates the round-the-world voyages of Sir Francis Drake, Captain James Cook and Sir Francis Chichester. Other memorials commemorate the passage of Halley's Comet and the work of the British Intelligence Services. Elsewhere are several military memorials at which wreath-laying ceremonies are occasionally held.

A LIVING CHURCH

THE VISIT DESCRIBED in this booklet has inevitably concentrated on the Abbey's history and artistic treasures, but you will also have seen that this is a working church. The Abbey's primary mission is to serve God through the offering of worship. In addition it strives to serve the Sovereign, the nation and all who visit here as tourists or pilgrims.

The Abbey has a distinctive role within the Church of England. It is neither a cathedral nor a parish church and stands outside the normal jurisdiction of bishops and archbishops. It is instead a Royal Peculiar, the status granted to it in 1560 by a charter of Elizabeth I, under which the Dean and Chapter are directly answerable to The Queen (FIG. 31).

The daily services sung and said here are only one part of the Abbey's work, for there are also many 'special' services and other events throughout the year. They include memorial services for distinguished public figures, services to mark significant occasions and annual events such as the Commonwealth Day Observance. Coronations are by their nature infrequent (there have been thirty-eight since 1066), but there have been many royal weddings (FIG. 32) and funerals here over the years, and

31 HM The Queen attends a special service in the Abbey

33 The Queen's Window by David Hockney (2018). It celebrates the reign of Queen Elizabeth II

the Abbey frequently provides a focus for the nation in times of national celebration or mourning. The commemoration in memorial tablets or stained glass of notable public figures has continued too, but burials in the Abbey are now very infrequent and only the interment of ashes is permitted.

The variety of the Abbey's life surprises many visitors. In addition to the organisation and conduct of its worship and music

32 The wedding of the Duke and Duchess of Cambridge, 2011

the Abbey runs a choir school, a shop, gardens, a library and archive, a museum, and a café. It also hosts many concerts, lectures and discussions. The work of caring for and conserving the fabric of the building never ends, and every year we welcome over a million visitors, the majority from overseas. All this requires a team of skilled staff – the Abbey currently employs 350 people and an army of valued volunteers.

Running the Abbey costs a great deal of money, and it is entirely self-supporting financially. It is for this reason that we ask our visitors to pay an admission charge. People sometimes feel uncomfortable about this, but the Abbey receives no income from the UK government, from the Church of England or from The Crown, and such charges are vital if this historic building is to be properly maintained so that future generations may use and appreciate it as we do. No one is ever charged to pray or to attend a service.

God is worshipped daily in the Abbey at four services (five on Sundays). The dean and canons, like the monks before them, maintain the regular services and invite others to worship here with them (FIG. 34). The Abbey's worship is often led by the choir, particularly in the evening, and the singing of the service allows worshippers to let their hearts and minds be carried away in the search of God. Each repetition of the daily liturgy confronts us with the challenge to human standards presented by the gospels and allows us to rediscover the wisdom contained in the Bible.

Today's world, in which belief and membership of the Church are regarded more as matters of personal choice than they once were, is very different from that of the kings, monks, masons and artists whose vision brought this building into being. But through the regular rythym of our daily worship and the many activities it organises, the Abbey continues to bring human life and God's purposes together in times of both joy and sadness. It remains an important part of the Church's role to encourage people, whatever their belief and whatever skills they possess, to see all life in the light of God's eternity.

God may be addressed at any time and in any words, but the discipline of certain times and particular words often helps. We therefore offer you a simple prayer, attributed to St Benedict, which you may wish to use yourself.

34 A visiting choir sings at a special service in the Abbey

O gracious and holy Father,
Give us wisdom to perceive you,
Diligence to seek you,
Patience to wait for you,
Eyes to behold you,
A heart to meditate upon you,
And a life to proclaim you,
Through the power of the
Spirit of Jesus Christ our Lord.
Amen.

This edition © Scala Arts & Heritage Publishers Ltd, 2013
Photography © Westminster Abbey Enterprises Ltd, 2013, except p.29 © Press Association
Text © Dean and Chapter of Westminster, 2013

First published in 2013 by Scala Arts & Heritage Publishers Ltd
10 Lion Yard, Tremadoc Road London SW4 7NQ

The text is a revised and updated version of an original text first published under the same title in 2006.

Reprinted 2019

ISBN 978 1 85759 820 9

Editor: Esme West
Proofreader: Julie Pickard
Designer: Nigel Soper
Printed and bound in China

Service Times

SUNDAYS
08.00 Holy Communion
10.00 Matins
11.00 Sung Eucharist (in St Margaret's Church)
11.15 Sung Eucharist
15.00 Evensong
18.30 Evening Service

WEEKDAYS
07.30 Matins (09.00 on Bank Holidays)
08.00 Holy Communion
12.30 Holy Communion
17.00 Evensong (said service on Wednesdays)

SATURDAYS
08.00 Holy Communion
09.00 Matins
15.00 Evensong (17.00 in summer)

Visitors are always welcome at these services. The above times may alter when other events take place. Please check the Abbey's website or telephone for the latest information.

Westminster Abbey
London SW1P 3PA
Email: info@westminster-abbey.org
www.westminster-abbey.org
Tel.: (020) 7222 5152

FRONT COVER: A view of the nave looking west from the organ loft

BACK COVER: The west towers of Westminster Abbey

BACK COVER FLAP: The nave vaulting

INSIDE BACK COVER: The nave looking west